MORNING MANNA MEDITATIONS

VOLUME II

Facing Adversity With Victory In View

MORNING MANNA MEDITATIONS
VOLUME II
Facing Adversity With Victory In View

Thomasine T. Wortham, Ph.D.

Inspirational Publications
Flint, Michigan

All scripture quotations, unless otherwise indicated, are taken from the *New King James Version*®. Copyright © 1987 by Thomas Nelson, Inc. Used following Gratis Use Guidelines. All rights reserved.

Scripture quotations taken from the Holy Bible, *NEW INTERNATIONAL VERSION*®, NIV® Copyright © 1973, 1978, 1984, 2011 by Biblica, Inc.® Used following Gratis Use Guidelines. All rights reserved worldwide.

Copyright ©2020 Thomasine T. Wortham, Ph.D.

All Rights Reserved.

ISBN: 978-1-7359912-0-7

No part of this book may be reproduced or transmitted in any form or by any means; graphic, electronic, or mechanical, including photocopying, recording, taping or by any information storage retrieval system without written permission of the author.

Author: Thomasine T. Wortham, Ph.D.
Author Email: twortham@gtmusa.org
Author Website: www.gtmusa.org

Manuscript Design and Published by: Inspirational Publications
Kimberly M. Broome, Consultant

Cover: www.shutterstock.com
Printed By: IngramSpark/USA

Printed in the United States of America

Table of Contents

Dedication 7
Acknowledgements 8
Introduction 10
A Conquering Spirit 13
A Forward Focus 15
A Mighty Ally 17
A Season of Sifting 19
Anchored 21
The Arm of the LORD 23
Battle Ready 25
Call Him 27
Care Not 29
Cry Out! 31
Cry Out! II 33
Faith for the Day 35
Faith is a Choice 37
Faith Works 39
Fear Not! 41
Handling Hardship 43
Called into His Rest 45
I Trust 47
Mount Up 49
My Help 51

My Portion	53
Never Give Up	55
Quiet Confidence	57
Relief Please!	59
Rescue 911	61
Safe in Him	63
The Secret Place	65
Stand Firm	67
Stand Still	69
Steadfast Faith	71
Tempted Yet Triumphant I	73
Tempted Yet Triumphant II	75
Tempted Yet Triumphant III	77
The Quiet Soul	79
The Refiner's Fire	81
Trust During Trouble	83
Under the Shelter	85
Unshakeable	87
When the Storm Rises	89
When Trouble Comes	91
Wilderness Seasons	93
Reflections	95

Dedication

With a heart overflowing with love, appreciation, and gratitude, I dedicate this work to the enduring memory and legacy of my mother, Shirley Ann Thornton (Mommy), who took her rest in the arms of the Lord December 27, 1996.

When I think of adversity, I am reminded of how courageous you were to give birth to me at 15 years old, especially being a Black girl in the Commonwealth of Virginia. I cannot imagine the rejection, shame, and fear you must have faced. Married at 15 and divorced before the age of 17, you never stopped working, never stopped loving people, and never failed to let others know how proud you were of me. It has always been my heart desire for you to be proud of me, and I believe you would be proud of this work.

One of my clearest memories is that you absolutely LOVED to read and learn. I am confident that from you I inherited your fighting spirit, love for people, love for knowledge, love for laughter, and love for reading. I believe that if you could read this book, you would pause, smile, and say, *"My baby wrote this!"*

I love you, Mommy, and I miss you so much! Thank you for your sacrifice for me, your confidence in me, and for always being proud of me!

Acknowledgements

The list is endless of people who have inspired, encouraged, and motivated me to write, enabling me to finally persevere and begin to use this gift to bless others. I could never name them all. Some have prayed, purchased the first volume of Morning Manna Meditations, and nudged me to continue writing. I am eternally grateful for the many ways in which you have extended and demonstrated your love and support.

My husband, Pastor Woody (aka "Woody My Honey") is always there to refresh me and love me unconditionally. I am increasingly amazed at his capacity to love and especially his desire to support my dreams. Thank You, Lord, for placing me in his heart and for prompting him to come and find me. Woody my honey, I pray that God graces us with many, many more years to fulfill our individual and joined purposes for His glory!

There is a beautiful new bouquet that God placed in my life in the person of my editor and publisher, Kimberly Broome. Her beautiful spirit, love for the Lord, creativity, and giftedness facilitated the publication of this devotional. The patience, wisdom, and insight that she provided were always offered with grace and love. Who knew that God was gifting me with another precious sister in the Lord as well as an excellent resource to help me fulfill my God-given assignment? Of course, HE knew! Thank you, Kim! You are a priceless gem! I love you!

Finally, it is my ultimate joy to acknowledge my loving Heavenly Father, who is the giver of "every good and perfect gift" (James 1:17). I am humbled by Your grace that enables me and Your mercy that forgives my delays and detours. Thank You, Lord for trusting me to be a good steward of the gifts that You have entrusted to me.

Many thanks to each of you for your love and support! May each reading empower, encourage, and equip you to see only victory as you navigate the storms of life!

Introduction

Adversity, trouble, crisis, affliction, or tribulation, by whatever name, is unwelcome and untimely. Nevertheless, it enters everyone's life in some form or another. When adversity comes, we may experience a range of emotions and thoughts including anger, hopelessness, helplessness, isolation, and fear, to name a few. Although these are normal human emotions, we must not allow our emotions to determine how we navigate the trouble. You may believe that no one understands or even feel like God has abandoned you; but there is evidence to the contrary. During these times of weakness, you can take comfort in knowing that God is with you and that Jesus understands your experience. The words, attributed to the Apostle Paul, confirm the truth that Christ can relate to our hardships:

> *"Therefore, since we have a great high priest who has gone through the heavens, Jesus the Son of God, let us hold firmly to the faith we profess. For we do not have a high priest who is unable to sympathize with our weaknesses, but we have one who has been tempted in every way, just as we are—yet was without sin. Let us then approach the throne of grace with confidence, so that we may receive mercy and find grace to help us in our time of need." Hebrews 4:14-16*

This book is an inspirational and practical tool designed to provide knowledge, strength, and encouragement, particularly for the stormy seasons in our lives. For the next 40 days, set your focus on God's love, grace, protection, presence, and the victory that Jesus won for you through His death on the cross. Each daily writing offers encouragement from the Word of God to stir your faith and to motivate you to face adversity with courage and hope. As you embark upon this faith-building journey, believe that your trouble will end in victory. Before you begin your daily reading ask the Lord to show you how to apply the message to your life. At the end of each reading, spend a few "manna moments" reflecting and completing the exercise provided.

I pray that your faith, joy, and peace increase each day as you learn to face adversity as a victorious child of the Living God!

Thomasine T. Wortham, Ph.D.
Grace Transformational Ministries, Inc.

A Conquering Spirit

"Who shall separate us from the love of Christ? Shall tribulation, or distress, or persecution, or famine, or nakedness, or peril, or sword? As it is written: "For Your sake we are killed all day long; We are accounted as sheep for the slaughter." Yet in all these things we are more than conquerors through Him who loved us."

Romans 8:35-37 NKJV

How do you view yourself, as a chump or a champ? Without a doubt, God says you are a victor and a champion! He wants you to see yourself as one who overcomes every challenge and conquers every foe. This perspective is necessary to live a victorious life. These days call for a conquering spirit. Without this kind of mind-set, the situations that we face could become overwhelming causing one to have a defeatist view. Paul, the apostle, reminds us of who we are – that we are MORE THAN CONQUERORS. To say that we are "more than conquerors" emphasizes the level of victory that God desires for us.

A conqueror is one who overcomes, subdues, and defeats whatever comes his or her way. You could say that a conqueror always comes out on top. When an enemy appears, the conqueror overthrows it and gains the victory. God says that YOU are MORE than a conqueror regardless of the enemy that you face. You have the power to master whatever mountain stands before you. During trouble or hardship, take courage in the fact that it cannot separate you from the love of Christ. That is very comforting! In times of hardship, stop and remind yourself of this truth. Stop and think about what this means. If the hardship cannot separate you from His love, this means that HE is in the hardship with you. If HE is in the hardship with you, then you will SURELY come out on top. Being more than a conqueror must mean that you exceed whatever level other conquerors reach. Imagine that!!! You, because of Christ, are an EXTREME CHAMPION! Glory to God!!

What should you do then in time of hardship or trouble? You should focus on the power of God's love for you. Meditate on that love and take ownership of it. Say continually, "God loves me. I receive that love, and I will hold on to it." Look for opportunities to express God's love to people. This helps to re-focus your mind off the trouble and hardship. God's love enables you to go THROUGH trouble with an attitude of victory and a conquering spirit.

MANNA MOMENT: List at least 7 qualities of a conquering spirit. Resolve today to develop these qualities.

A Forward Focus

"Let your eyes look straight ahead, and your eyelids look right before you. Ponder the path of your feet and let all your ways be established. Do not turn to the right or the left; remove your foot from evil."

Proverbs 4:25-27 NKJV

Focus is a major key to successful living. If we are to fulfill the purposes and callings that God has for our lives, the ability to focus must be mastered. Focus requires that your attention be set and that you not be distracted or moved from your focal point. This requires the ability to lock in on a point of concentration. When focus is broken, progress is lost, and momentum is weakened. As a result, more energy is required to regain ground that was already covered. So, be alert to potential distractions that may cause broken focus.

There are many things that have the potential of breaking our focus. We can be distracted by losses, relationship issues, financial problems, the desire for fun, fatigue, and many other factors. Thank God that Scripture teaches us how to maintain focus. The answer to maintaining focus lies in where you look. Fix your physical and spiritual eyes on what lies ahead, or you will succumb to distractions. When you set a goal, do not look around or behind you. The goal is in front of you and that is where you must fix your gaze. If you are to maintain your focus, you must think very deliberately about where you plant your feet. Every step counts, and you do not want to waste time or energy. The thing that you focus on is what becomes largest in your view. Keep looking forward at all costs. Keep your spiritual eyes open through prayer and study of the Word of God. Doing so will equip you to recognize evil and whatever may come to cause you to look behind you or to the left or to the right.

When you decide to set your focus on God's Word and on His purpose for your life, countless opportunities to turn will appear. You will be tempted to take turns that will not lead to the purpose that God has for your life. Some roads will look very appealing and may look like they will lead where God is directing you. Beware!! Do not be deceived. Stay on the path. Do not look down those side roads. Stop and think, and the Holy Spirit will help you to see how those roads might lead you astray. The Word of God is your road map to keep you on the right path. Look ahead! Keep your eyes on Jesus and stay on the road that leads to life.

MANNA MOMENT: What are the current distractions in your life? How will you overcome them?

A Mighty Ally

"The Lord is on my side; I will not fear. What can man do to me? The Lord is with me; he is my helper. I will look in triumph on my enemies."

Psalm 118:6 NKJV

"So, we say with confidence, "The Lord is my helper; I will not be afraid. What can man do to me?"

Hebrews 13:6 NIV

"If you love Me, keep My commandments. And I will pray the Father, and He will give you another Helper, that He may abide with you forever—the Spirit of truth, whom the world cannot receive, because it neither sees Him nor knows Him; but you know Him, for He dwells with you and will be in you."

John 14:15-16 NIV

Who really likes to think about having enemies? Typically, no one, but they are present, nonetheless – spiritual and physical enemies. The physical enemies are being influenced by the spiritual enemies, which are Satan and his agents. The enemy of your soul is the catalyst for every attack that comes against you, but he is defeated along with all his works. The works of the enemy come in many forms with the intent of causing you to lose faith in what God has done for you through His Son, Jesus Christ. The initial response when faced with an enemy is typically to fear. Therefore, you must immediately declare as David often did, "I WILL NOT FEAR!" Even if you feel the emotion of fear, the declaration should be, "I will not embrace this fear!" This declaration positions you to stand in faith against your enemies. Your stance now becomes one of faith. Victory is certain when you put your trust in the Lord.

Remember that you have a MIGHTY ally, the Lord God Almighty. He is on your side just as the psalmist says (see Psalm 118:6). He is standing with you against your enemy. The Lord is your Helper; therefore, you are never alone (Hebrews 13:6). With God on your side, you can count on the Holy Spirit, your Helper, (see John 14:15-16). Whether the enemies are people who intend to do your harm or a health issue, financial problem, marital problem, etc. the help (strength) of the Lord is with you. Declare with confidence "The Lord is my helper; I will not be afraid." When you proclaim that the Lord is your helper, you stir up your confidence and remind yourself of the SOURCE of your help. The Maker of the heavens and the earth has teamed up with you against your adversaries. You cannot be overcome by man when the Lord of Hosts goes before you and is aligned with you in the battle. So then, do not retreat from your enemies face them with all confidence and boldness knowing that you have A MIGHTLY ALLY who goes before you. HE is the one who lives within you, and the one who is your rear guard.

MANNA MOMENT: Identify any enemies that have caused you to retreat. Now declare that the Lord is with you and ADVANCE to your place of victory!

A Season of Sifting

"And the Lord said, "Simon, Simon! Indeed, Satan has asked for you, that he may sift you as wheat."

Luke 22:31 NKJV

Jesus warned Simon Peter of a day that would come when his faith would be greatly tested. Peter could not imagine that he would ever come to the place of denying his Lord. The thought was too much for him to fathom. Like Peter, we often come to points in our lives where we face the unimaginable and find ourselves making decisions that we would never have thought possible. These may be times that Satan intends to "sift you as wheat." (Luke 22:31) Peter found himself in a season of sifting, and but for the prayers of the Lord Jesus, he would not have recovered. Did you know that Jesus is interceding for you during your time of temptation? (see Hebrews 7:25). You do not have to be sifted like wheat!

When wheat is sifted, it is filtered, shaken, and thrashed to separate it from the chaff. According to the Bible, the Lord Jesus will determine the proper time for separating the wheat from the tares. However, Satan desired to separate Simon Peter from his place of security in Christ and cause him to walk away permanently. Although Peter experienced the anguishing pain of having denied his Lord, the devil could not destroy Peter's relationship with Christ. Because of the love that Christ had for Peter, He was moved with compassion to pray for Peter's faith to be strong enough to withstand the test. When the moment of sifting came, Peter failed, but he was smitten in his heart and repented.

Jesus knew that Peter would deny Him, but He also knew that Peter would repent. Knowing this, He charged Peter to strengthen his brothers during their times of temptation. After experiencing the sorrow of denying the Savior and turning his heart back on Christ, Peter would use that failure to build up his brothers. Peter by the grace of God, overcame the shame and guilt and went on to obey the command to fortify his brothers. We continue to be strengthened by the work of Peter and by words of grace that he penned by inspiration of the Holy Spirit.

Every believer has or will face a moment of sifting ... moments when we know we have failed Christ. God forbid that we should deny Him or walk away from the faith. When sifting comes, we are tempted to doubt His promises. At these times remember that Jesus is praying FOR YOU. According to Hebrew 7:25, Jesus will forever intercede for you so that your faith will not fail. After you come through your season of sifting, help your weaker brother.

MANNA MOMENT: If you are in a season of sifting, turn, repent, so that your faith will not fail. Identify two people that you will help today and encourage them to keep the faith!

Anchored

"This hope we have as an anchor of the soul, both sure and steadfast, and which enters the Presence behind the veil, where the forerunner has entered for us, even Jesus, having become High Priest forever according to the order of Melchizedek."

Hebrews 6:19-20 NKJV

"Why are you cast down, O my soul? And why are you disquieted within me? Hope in God, for I shall yet praise Him. For the help of His countenance."

Psalm 42:5 NKJV

What do you hold onto when it looks like everything around you is falling apart? When God's promises and purposes for your life seem like impossibilities, how will you remain solid in your Christian walk? When everything meaningful seems beyond your grasp, what will keep you secure? What will give you stability in a world that appears to be becoming more wicked and more irreverent every day? How will your soul remain stable and fixed on the promises and plans that God ordained for your life? Well, the answer is HOPE – EXPECTATION.

The Bible declares that we have a hope that can keep the soul intact so that we remain steadfast in our position of faith. You see, without hope the elements of the soul (the mind, will, and emotions) may be tossed in all directions. We can become unstable and even downcast like the psalmist. It is a blessing to know that God has given His promises and HIS oath so that we can be secure in our position in

Him. Scripture reveals those two things cannot change. God has given us so many valuable promises and has guaranteed the certainty of them by giving us His oath. He swore by Himself, and He CANNOT lie. Consequently, we can hold onto everything that God has said and without wavering, following the example of Abraham.

There will be times when we are tempted to stagger concerning God's promises, but we look at Abraham who refused to stumble at God's Word (Romans 4:20). Abraham hoped when there was NO REASON to hope. He just believed God! He expected God to keep His promise. Similarly, when the psalmist realized that he was downtrodden in his soul, He challenged his soul to re-direct his hope back to God. We must do the same when our souls begin to flounder from the place of stability. If we will hold onto this strong and reliable hope, we can enter the presence of God with confidence. As the Scripture says, Jesus has already gone ahead and prepared the way for us. Even in this present age, our souls can remain safe and sound, because our hope is in HIM!

MANNA MOMENT: Assess the stability of your soul. Is it downcast, discouraged, or in despair? Record what you discovered. Re-direct your hope to the source, the true and living God.

The Arm of the LORD

"Oh, sing to the Lord a new song! For He has done marvelous things, His right hand and His holy arm have gained Him the victory."

Psalm 98:1 NKJV

God has done more marvelous things for us than we can count! During times of adversity, take time to reflect on those wonderful things. Can you find a song during troubled times? The psalmist admonishes us to sing a new song to the Lord and explains why we should sing. The fact that the Lord has done extraordinary things for us should evoke a song from the heart. We have victory because of God's mercy and faithfulness. Singing about His goodness and faithfulness is a way that we express our gratitude. When we do this during times of hardship, faith arises in our hearts, and we delight the heart of God! This brings up memories of past victories and of the One who brought us through.

Victory never comes from the arm of flesh, but rather from the ARM OF THE LORD. The term "arm of the Lord" is symbolic for His strength, might, or power, which when applied (or stretched out) on our behalf empowers us to overcome and triumph over our enemies. Make no mistake about the source of your victory. It did not come from the arm of man, but from the HOLY arm of God. The strength (arm) of the Lord differs in nature from other forms of power. The Lord's arm (strength) is sacred, pure, and is full of virtue. He demonstrated His might through holy power that has no impurities because it is motivated by love in its purest form.

When God stretches out His arm concerning you, as He did with the children of Israel, it is unmistakable that He is the source of the victory. Jesus demonstrated the power of the arm of the Lord through His death, burial, and resurrection. Christ won the victory over sin and the grave for us all and specifically, for YOU. The faithful, holy love of God worked on our behalf, conquering death, hell, and the grave. Because of God's Holy arm, all can enter the victory that Christ won on the Cross of Calvary. The ARM OF THE LORD has defeated every enemy. No enemy can stand against you in the presence of the outstretched arm of the Lord.

MANNA MOMENT: Identify the enemies that oppose you and ask the Lord God to stretch out HIS HOLY ARM on your behalf. Then watch your enemies scatter.

Battle Ready

"Blessed be the Lord my Rock, who trains my hands for war, and my fingers for battle. My loving-kindness and my fortress, my high tower and my deliverer, my shield and the One in whom I take refuge, who subdues my people under me."

Psalm 144:1-2 NKJV

King David was a man who was well acquainted with war. He was a skilled warrior who experienced many victories in battle. In fact, King David was familiar with both physical and spiritual warfare. In this writing, he offers praise to God for the victories that he has experienced and gives credit to God for his skill in battle. This prophet, priest, and king was extraordinarily deliberate in acknowledging who God had been to him. This is one of David's greatest strengths – that he KNEW his God. When you know your God, you can take comfort in that knowledge and expect to experience victory. David knew God as:

- Rock – Strength, stabilizer
- Fortress – Refuge, shelter
- High Tower – Stronghold, place of security
- Deliverer – the One who brings him to safety
- Shield – Protection, guard

This warrior had an understanding and revelation that all his skill came from the Lord. King David recognized that it was the loving-kindness and goodness of the Lord that sustained him in battle. Every victory resulted from the ability given to him by God.

Whenever this warrior was in battle, he experienced God as his Rock, his Fortress, his Stronghold, his Deliverer, and his Shield. That is what kept him safe. When you are engaged in battle, you can count on God to subdue your enemies. Whether you are engaged in the horrible reality of war like David or whether it is a spiritual battle, know that GOD IS YOUR ROCK. He is with you whether the enemies are physical or spiritual. Intimate knowledge of HIM will enable you to maintain your faith during any battle.

David willingly submitted to the instruction and training of the Lord. He revered the precepts, commands, and statutes of the Lord. Victory was possible because of David's willingness to hear and obey. God will give direction and guidance during the heat of battle. Your obedience to these commands, will determine your level of victory. Listen, obey, and watch God subdue your enemies.

MANNA MOMENT: What instruction is God giving you concerning your current battle? Write them down and follow them to the letter.

Call Him

"This is what the LORD says, He who made the earth, the LORD who formed it and established it—the LORD is his name: 'Call to Me and I will answer you and tell you great and unsearchable things you do not know."

Jeremiah 33:2-3 NKJV

Throughout scripture, there are examples of people calling upon the Lord. In these instances, we see patterns of the LORD answering those cries. God has a track record of responding when we call upon Him. There is no need for concern about getting a response from God because He will never ignore you. This is unlike the response that may be received from people. Sometimes you may call upon someone who is unavailable, or they simply cannot hear you. Some may even choose to not answer the call. What a comfort is it to know that the Lord is always available; He is never out of earshot and will always pay attention to your call. The sound of your voice is pleasing unto God, and He takes pleasure is responding to you.

The Lord knows the reason for your call even before you utter a sound. In addition, He is ready to move on your behalf and act. The Bible reveals that when you call upon the Lord:

- He will hear you. 2 Samuel 22:7
- He will answer you. Psalm 18:3; Psalm 27:7
- He will share amazing things with you. Jeremiah 33:2-3
- He will save you from your enemies. 2 Samuel 22:4

These are but a few of the ways that God responds to the voice of His children. Deliverance comes when you call upon His name. Circumstances change when the cries of the righteous reach the ears of the Lord. Your voice activates God's involvement in your affairs and that brings about radical changes in your situation. When King David was in distress, he was quick to call upon the God of his salvation and he was always confident that God would answer. He had cultivated a habit of involving God in his life. Because of this, he developed a series of testimonies of how God acted on his behalf. Do you have a habit of calling unto the Lord early during your distress? Has He answered your call for mercy, help, or deliverance from your enemies? If so, then know that He will do it again and again! If you have not called upon Him in the past, why not start with your current dilemma and watch God show you things that you cannot imagine?

MANNA MOMENT: Take time to revisit the ways that God responded to your previous calls for help.

Care Not

"Therefore, humble yourselves under the mighty hand of God, that He may exalt you in due time, casting all your care upon Him, for He cares for you."

1 Peter 4:6-7 NKJV

"*I* Don't Care!" This ought to be the declaration of every believer. This is not a statement of apathy nor is it one of callousness. When you proclaim that you do not care it does not mean that you are disconnected from reality or that you are out of touch with what is happening. Peter, the apostle, tells you what you should do with "care." He says, "cast them." That means to throw them off, to get rid of, or to discard them. Cares should be far from the believer. There are always opportunities to fret or be anxious, so you must repeatedly say to yourself, "I do not care." Make this announcement to the devil and to yourself. Say, "I will NOT care! I will pray!"

The Bible instructs us to cast our cares. It says you should cast them on HIM because He cares for you. You have a place to throw those cares. You can throw them on the Lord because HE can and will handle them. In fact, Jesus died for you to be "care-FREE". You are on God's mind so whatever is going on in your life is in HIS thoughts. Therefore, you need not worry. Why be entangled in worry and fear when you have a place to place those cares? God is well able to handle anything that you cast off. On the other hand, you are completely incapable of changing ANYTHING by worrying. Nothing changes when you worry, but EVERYTHING can change when you shed those cares by giving them to the Lord. At the very least, YOU will be different!

God cares for you. Not only does He care for YOU, but HE also cares *in* your place. You have a heavenly Father who bears your burdens so that you can live a stress-free life. You have been relieved of the cares of this life and granted permission to throw every issue upon Him. Humble yourself by acknowledging your inadequacies and your dependence upon Him. Tell God how much you need Him and that you need His grace (enabling power) to increase in your life so that you can live "care-FREE." Continue to boldly say, "I do not care!" ... not out of anger or frustration, but from a position of faith because you have permission to live without a care.

MANNA MOMENT: Make a list of cares that you will cast upon the Lord.

Cry Out!

"Lord, how they have increased who trouble me! Many are they who rise up against me. Many are they who say of me, "There is no help for him in God." Selah. But You, O Lord, are a shield for me, My glory and the One who lifts up my head."

Psalm 3:1-3 NKJV

King David was acquainted with both victory and failure. He had public victories as well as public failures. There was no shortage of people around him to remind him of those failures. When people operate according to natural tendencies and fail to operate in the compassion of the Lord, they will be quick to point out the failures of others. They may view themselves and others in light of past failures. King David knew what it was like to receive accolades from men, but he was also acquainted with contempt and disdain from his enemies. In either situation, David's pattern was to turn to the Lord God Almighty in prayer, praise, and worship. This psalm demonstrates David's pattern of going to the Lord to seek peace, comfort, and refuge, which always led to victory.

Notice the process that David followed to arrive at the place of victory. He began with laying his situation before God with complete openness and specificity. There was no pretense; he outlined the reality of the situation before God. He set his focus on God with full faith and acknowledgment of who God was to him. God was David's shield, and he knew that because of the many times that God has protected him in military battle. This battle would be no different. David was certain that God would restore him to a place of honor (lift his head). Then David CRIED unto the Lord and the Lord HEARD him. Crying out to God was a critical facet of David's relationship with the Lord. He was never ashamed to cry out with a loud voice unto the God of His salvation. After that, David slept and woke up without fear. Hallelujah! Peace came, and David declared that it was because the LORD SUSTAINED HIM! Finally, David cried again for salvation – deliverance – and reflected on God's history of rescuing him from all his enemies. He affirmed that God was His source of salvation and blessing. This process is not just for David. It worked for him, and it will work for you. Engage now!

MANNA MOMENT: Walk through the process that David used and *CRY OUT!*

Cry Out! II

"Now it happened in the process of time that the king of Egypt died. Then the children of Israel groaned because of the bondage, and they cried out; and their cry came up to God because of the bondage. So, God heard their groaning, and God remembered His covenant with Abraham, with Isaac, and with Jacob. And God looked upon the children of Israel, and God acknowledged them."

Exodus 2:23-25 NKLV

God hears the cries of His people. In this account from the Old Testament, the Israelites were in a desperate situation. They were enslaved, overburdened with work, and abused. Their response to these conditions was to cry out to God. When the people cried out to the Lord, God gave them His attention. He did not ignore them but rather responded to their call for help. God wants to do the same for you. He wants you to cry out to Him during your situation.

The Israelites were under the cruel hand of Pharaoh until the time of his death. They suffered under the control of this hard, cruel taskmaster for many years. This group of people experienced horrible oppression, but one day they did something different. They went to God in desperation. Perhaps they had cried out before, but something must have been different about this cry. Something happened when they cried out to God this time. Their cry activated the process of deliverance. They acted and so did God. All they did was cry out. That is the first step in the process. You must call on the Lord. Cry out and ask Him for help. In other words, you are the catalyst for your deliverance. Your desperate cry makes all the difference.

Notice that God moved into an action mode AFTER the people cried out. Look at what God did. He heard, remembered, looked upon them, and acknowledged them. If you cry out, God will hear you. He promised Abraham that He would bless those who blessed him and curse those who cursed him. That is the covenant that He remembered.

God is still faithful to that covenant and the promises include you. You can count on God to acknowledge you when you cry out. He WILL take notice of you. God will not disregard your call. Finally, God will recognize your voice and reply to your plea. He WILL answer, and that answer comes in the form of help. Your cry is precious to Him, and He is affected by your need. He is ready to change your situation. Take that step and cry out. Call on the Lord and watch Him move into action on your behalf.

MANNA MOMENT: Reflect upon times when God responded to your cries and give thanks to Him. Cry out to Him afresh today.

Faith for the Day

"But seek first the kingdom of God and His righteousness, and all these things shall be added to you. Therefore, do not worry about tomorrow, for tomorrow will worry about its own things. Sufficient for the day is its own trouble."

Matthew 6:33-34 NKJV

What is your first thought when you awake in the morning? Is it one that is full of faith and hope or is it of worry and fear? If it is the latter, then decide that today you will receive and operate in *"Faith for the Day."* Decide to set your mind on faith and not fear. The Bible informs us that if we pursue God above all else, then we have no need to worry or fear. The message from the Word of God is to live in "today" and not be drawn into the possible scenarios of what tomorrow may bring. So often, we miss the joys of today by being anxious about what may happen tomorrow. Has not God promised that when tomorrow comes, He will take care of our needs? This promise includes any issue that we may face. Knowing that His promise is true should bring a sense of ease, cause you to simply believe that you can rest and not fear.

Each day presents the opportunity to choose faith or fear. You have the option to follow either the path of faith or the path of fear. Choosing faith is simply a decision to trust and rely upon God and rest on His promises. When you choose to fear, you decide to trust what you see, hear, taste, touch, and smell. In other words, when you choose fear, it is like saying, "I have to rely on my senses" because they are more dependable than God. How dangerous it is to live even one day trusting more in your physical senses than on the faithfulness of God? When you choose faith, you acknowledge that God is more reliable than your senses and greater than anything or anyone in Heaven or earth. Fear generates questions about God's character. On the other hand, faith demonstrates confidence in God's reputation. So, begin each day – with a firm resolve to trust God no matter what the day holds. After all, we know who holds the day! Do not forfeit the precious moments of today with thoughts of fear, worry, or anxiety. When God awakens you each morning, seek Him and receive *"Faith for the Day."*

MANNA MOMENT: Make a firm decision to begin each day with "faith thoughts." Record 5 "faith thoughts" and let them position you for the day.

Faith is a Choice

"Now Thomas, called the Twin, one of the twelve, was not with them when Jesus came. The other disciples therefore said to him, "We have seen the Lord." So he said to them, "Unless I see in His hands the print of the nails, and put my finger into the print of the nails, and put my hand into His side, I will not believe."

John 20:24-25 NKJV

Faith is the key to everything concerning our relationship with God. It is the necessary ingredient if we are to have eternal life. Doubt hinders us from fully walking in the blessings of our salvation. In this account, Thomas was refusing to believe that Jesus had appeared to the other eleven disciples. He made a firm statement with conditions that had to be met for him to believe. He resolved that he would not believe 'UNTIL." He needed evidence before he would believe …touching the wounds of Jesus and putting his hand into Jesus' pierced side. He placed conditions on his faith. Later Jesus appears and gives him the opportunity to touch the wounds. Then Jesus rebuked him for needing to see before believing. Jesus further said that the blessed ones are those that believe WITHOUT seeing.

Are you believing for something that has not happened? Are you tempted to doubt because there is no physical evidence that it will happen? Well even if there is no tangible evidence that it will happen, you can CHOOSE to believe. Do not allow the absence of natural evidence to cause you to doubt. Believing when there is no sign of the "thing" happening demonstrates your confidence in God.

Despite evidence to the contrary, remain confident. When you choose to have faith in God, it empowers to break free of the control of outward circumstances.

This scenario with Thomas clearly shows us that faith is within our power of choice. You can CHOOSE to believe. God has given you a free will, and that allows you to make your own decisions. God trusts you to believe without being forced. He has placed confidence in you and believes that you will choose to believe in Him. He wants you to have faith in Him even when there is nothing to touch or feel. The Lord wants you to believe His promises when there is no proof or natural evidence.

Faith is your evidence. Your Father desired that you would say the opposite of what Thomas said. He wants to hear you say, "I WILL BELIEVE!" When you cannot see or touch anything, He wants you to CHOOSE FAITH over doubt. He also understands that choosing to believe can be difficult, and He is with you in that struggle. Believing is what separates you from those who have no relationship with Him. YOU can choose to be one of the "blessed ones" who has not seen but believes.

MANNA MOMENT: What circumstances or conditions interfere with your ability to choose faith?

Faith Works

"What does it profit, my brethren, if someone says he has faith but does not have works? Can faith save him? If a brother or sister is naked and destitute of daily food, and one of you says to them, "Depart in peace, be warmed and filled," but you do not give them the things which are needed for the body, what does it profit? Thus also faith by itself, if it does not have works, is dead. But someone will say, "You have faith, and I have works." Show me your faith without your works, and I will show you my faith by my works. You believe that there is one God. You do well. Even the demons believe—and tremble! But do you want to know, O foolish man, that faith without works is dead? Was not Abraham our father justified by works when he offered Isaac his son on the altar? Do you see that faith was working together with his works, and by works faith was made perfect?"

James 2:14-23 NKJV

We cannot please God without faith (Hebrews 11:6). That is a spiritual truth set forth in the Word of God, but faith must be demonstrated. If faith is alive in our hearts, there should be external evidence. In other words, your faith should move you to action. Faith is to be expressed in the form of good works that glorify our Father in Heaven. This passage illustrates this point. If you have faith in your heart, and you ignore the needs of others; then your faith was of no benefit. On the other hand, if your faith motivates you and action is taken to impact that person's need, then the person in need is blessed and God is glorified.

There are those who can intellectually acknowledge that God "is" but who do not love or obey Him. So, their faith is dead. It does not produce fruit and is not accompanied by acts of love and obedience.

Abraham is cited as one whose faith was alive because it was followed by action. The faith of Abraham went far beyond a mere recognition that God existed. Abraham's faith moved him to an extraordinary level of obedience. He trusted God to the degree that he was willing to sacrifice his only son, Isaac. God recognized this uncommon trust and called Abraham His friend. In the end, Abraham was not required to offer up his son, because God provided a ram for the sacrifice. Abraham's faith produced fruit which is the case with true saving faith. Will not God also provide a ram in the bush for you, as you obey Him without restraint?

The Bible clearly teaches us that it is not works that saves us; however, genuine faith will always produce good works. It is through acts of obedience to God that our faith is brought to maturity. True faith in the heart works its way into your life. It moves you to show forth love and compassion and looks for ways to glorify God. *FAITH WORKS!*

MANNA MOMENT: What 3 actions will you add to your faith today?

Fear Not!

"For God has not given us a spirit of fear, but of power and of love and of a sound mind."

2 Timothy 1:7 NKJV

"There is no ear in love; but perfect love casts out fear, because fear involves torment. But he who fears has not been made perfect in love."

1 John 4:18 NIV

Do not fear. That is an order – direct order from the Lord God! Fear is a spirit that torments and cripples if we allow it to enter our soul. God warns us repeatedly to reject fear and to give it NO PLACE our lives. The very nature of fear is to demand more and more mental space so that it can paralyze and hinder us from living a life of freedom. Fear causes us to have a sense of dread, foreboding, anxiety, or expectation of harm. Those of us who have the Spirit of God are to operate with a spirit of power, love, and sound mind (2 Timothy 1:7). When we operate from a fear base, we are timid, anxious, and weak. We fail to operate in faith and therefore cannot please God (Hebrews 11:6). The Word of God produces faith which drives out fear.

God's word explains why we should not fear. First, we should not fear, because it is a spirit that does not come from God. Fear is from the devil and is an instrument of torment (1 John 4:18). Fear is void of love and is intended to hinder us from receiving the perfect love of God. Secondly, we should reject fear because God promised to be with us and to protect us from danger (Isaiah 43:1-3). He will not allow us to drown or be burned. Circumstances can seem so overwhelming that we feel like we are drowning. Life can be so intense that it feels like it will consume like fire, but God says, "I am with you!" Whatever your current circumstances may be, remember that God is with you. You are not alone! The MIGHTY ONE of Israel is with you. If you allow His perfect love to rule, it will consume the fear! God wants each of his children to live free of the torment and the punishment of fear. Just remember that He has redeemed you; called you by name, and you are His own dear child. Will He not take care of His own? *Fear Not!*

MANNA MOMENT: Meditate on what it means to receive the perfect love of God. Record 5 thoughts about how God's perfect love will cast fear out of your life.

Handling Hardship

"Many are the afflictions of the righteous, But the Lord delivers him out of them all."

Psalm 34:19 NKJV

How do you respond to adversity? Are you currently in the middle of an adverse situation, recovering from a crisis, or just entering a time of testing? Most people are in one of these modes. Adversity, affliction, suffering ... we all have our times of distress, which involve misfortune, pain, and suffering. When adversity comes, if you remember that the Lord, Our God, is a strong deliverer, you can face trouble with the assurance of victory. King David was a man who learned to face adversity. Whenever trouble came upon him, he would acknowledge the reality of the trouble, share his feelings with the Lord, and cry out for help from God. That is the model that you can follow when you are in any trouble. There is no virtue in denying the adversity, nor is it praiseworthy to ignore how trouble affects your soul. Be honest with God about your emotions.

Read through the Psalms and notice how David spoke honestly with God about his loneliness and pain. He was so confident in his relationship with God that he shared his REAL FEELINGS with the Lord. David expected the Lord to hear him and was bold in asking the Lord to rescue him. In your time of adversity, express your feelings to God. Empty out your soul before Him and cry out. Countless, times we hear King David say, "In my distress I cried unto to the Lord and He heard me." (Psalms 18:6; 55:17). In other words, he is saying when I was in trouble this is what worked for me. Would you dare to believe that if it worked for King David that it will work for you too? If you will handle adversity the way that he did, God will respond the way that He responded to this man of faith and courage.

The Word of God plainly states that those who are in right standing with God will have MANY adverse situations – much suffering; BUT those situations will not be permanent. The Lord will bring you to a place of safety whenever trouble comes. That is the confidence that you must develop. It may not appear that there is an end in sight, but there is a point of finality to the suffering. It lasts "a while" but deliverance comes. Know that God will transport you to a place of safety – a landing place where trouble cannot touch you.

MANNA MOMENT: Identify the current adversity in your life and relate to God the way that King David did in his times of distress. Share 3 specific things with God about this adversity. What was God's response?

Called into His Rest

"Come to Me, all you who labor and are heavy laden, and I will give you rest. Take My yoke upon you and learn from Me, for I am gentle and lowly in heart, and you will find rest for your souls. For My yoke is easy and My burden is light."

Matthew 11:28-30 NKJV

In today's world, rest is a need that is extremely neglected, yet it is vitally important. In scripture, we find times when Jesus takes his disciples "to the other side." He took them away from all the day-to-day activity where they could be refreshed and renewed. The demands of this age require us to be mindful of the need of rest for our bodies and souls. Life pressures can cause weariness and eventually cause us to faint unless we heed the call to rest. Jesus extends the open call to rest for all who will respond. This rest is characterized by peace of mind and heart, the absence of stressful labor, and the presence of refreshing. Even when we rest our physical bodies, our souls (mind, will, and emotions) continue to labor. Decisions to make, responsibilities to handle, or issues to resolve often compete with the peace that God wants us to enjoy.

We must learn to enter the rest that God offers for our souls. Jesus Himself tells us how to find this rest. Here is the process that He outlines: 1) Come to Me; 2) Learn of Me (get to know Me); and 3) Yoke up (walk/submit/serve) with Me. This process works every time. When we simply come to Him and commune with Him, become intimately acquainted with Him, and submit to His will, rest will be the reward. The yoke of Jesus is easy and brings no pressure.

His yoke is marked by peace, comfort, and the lack of struggle. His is a yoke of love. Jesus promised that if we become tired or burdened that He would GIVE us rest. That is His gift to us. We should simply respond to the call to come and receive His rest. Jesus is calling you to a place of rest today where you can enjoy a time of refreshing and peace. Will you STOP and respond to the call?

MANNA MOMENT: Identify 5 obstacles that hinder you from resting physically, emotionally, or spiritually.

I Trust

"Keep my soul, and deliver me; Let me not be ashamed, for I put my trust in You."

Psalms 25:20 NKJV

At the time that you are reading this, you may have been betrayed, disappointed, or rejected by someone in whom you had placed your trust. If not, it is safe to say that most of us have known the pain of having our trust abused or violated. Whether your disappointment is current or from a past incident, be assured that there is ONE who will never betray you. We sometimes trust the wrong people, or we may trust the right people but at the wrong time. Be reminded that you can trust God ALL THE TIME.

The Bible admonishes us to put our trust IN HIM and by doing so, He will lead us to the right people–people who are also trusting IN HIM. The pain of betrayed trust is deep and leaves us with the need to withdraw or move into modes of self-protection so that we will not be hurt again in that way. God never wants us to protect ourselves by living behind walls or putting up barriers that love cannot penetrate. He wants us to depend upon Him to shield us so that we can continue to freely give and receive love.

Trust is a matter of the heart which begins with reliance upon the Lord with ALL your heart. The Lord God wants the whole heart and He wants to be involved in ALL our affairs. Trust Him in every area, and He will lead you on the right path EVERY TIME and point you in the right direction –ALL THE TIME.

When the psalmist declares his trust in the Lord, he is declaring that the Lord is his safe place. When someone lets us down, we may lose trust and our sense of safety. Then we might begin to shield ourselves by closing our hearts to that person. Betrayal can also result in shame and embarrassment, particularly when the situation is public. We may become self-conscious and want to hide until the embarrassment passes or until people forget. Know this! You have a promise from God that you will NEVER be ashamed if you trust IN HIM. He will never abandon, reject, abuse, or betray you! Moreover, when you are hurt by others, He will be your refuge until the shame passes over! Is there any better place to put your trust than IN HIM?

MANNA MOMENT: Identify specific people who betrayed you or violated your trust and pray for them. Surrender to God and release all hurt, anger, fear, and resentment. Now spend quiet moments in the safety of His healing presence.

Mount Up

"Even youths grow tired and weary, and young men stumble and fall; but those who hope in the Lord will renew their strength. They will soar on wings like eagles; they will run and not grow weary; they will walk and not be faint."

Isaiah 40:30-31 NKJV

There are times when the winds of life may tempt you to give in to the weariness and fatigue that can result from a storm. You can become so overwhelmed with pressure that you may feel that your strength is being siphoned out of you. The Bible reveals that young and old are subject to weariness, and that the lack of strength can result in stumbling or even a fall. However, the Scripture goes on to give us the remedy for waning strength. That remedy is to hope in the Lord. This hope is an expectation and anticipation that is centered on the faithfulness of God. When you are in the midst of the storm you must remember that God is in the storm with you and that He will not abandon you during your time of trouble. The gusts of life are real; however, there is a truth that supersedes any turbulence that you will ever experience. That truth is that God will NEVER leave you nor forsake you (Hebrews 13:5b). When you know that God is with you during your trouble, your hope comes alive. This hope causes you to renew your strength and enable you to make the decision to *"MOUNT UP!"*

The Bible gives us a picture of what it means to *"MOUNT UP"* by using the example of the eagle, specifically the eagle's wings. The eagle has massive wings which serve this powerful bird of prey well, especially in times of a storm. While the average bird fears and takes cover in times of a storm, the eagle is quite different. The eagle looks for and uses the thermal winds of a storm to soar. That is what it means to "*MOUNT UP.*" When the right wind comes along, the eagle learns to use "the lift" of the thermal wind to soar above the storm. At this time, the eagle can cease from flapping his wings and simply spread those wings and soar above the stormy conditions down below. Could it be that it is time for you to stop flapping your wings (laboring) and find the wind that will lift you above the stormy circumstances of your life? You can renew (exchange) your strength so that you can run and walk without becoming overcome with fatigue. Look at the eagle and learn from the principle of the lift. Be renewed in strength. *MOUNT UP!*

MANNA MOMENT: The "lift" is coming! Take time to identify the current storm(s) that you are in and record how you will recognize and use the Lord's lift to rise above them.

My Help

"I will lift up my eyes to the hills—From whence comes my help? My help comes from the Lord, Who made heaven and earth.

Psalm 121:1-2 NKJV

"The Lord shall preserve you from all evil; He shall preserve your soul. The Lord shall preserve your going out and your coming in from this time forth, and even forevermore."

Psalm 121:7-8 NIV

"Our soul waits for the Lord; He is our help and our shield."

Psalm 33:20 NKJV

It is certain that in this life we will have trouble. Jesus made it at point to inform us that this world provide tribulation for the believer (John 16:33). There is no doubt that trouble is an inescapable reality, but we need not despair because Jesus has assured us that HE has overcome the world. Trouble comes in many forms and varies in duration. Trouble is much like pain. It can be acute, that is, short and severe; or it can be chronic, long, and lasting. Either one is undesirable. Trouble may come in the form of financial pressure, family problems, work pressures, relationship issues, or sickness and disease, just to name a few of life's challenges. No matter what form the trouble takes, it is safe to say that we need help when tribulation comes. It is also true that trouble is always unwelcome and always comes at the wrong time. When, (not if) trouble comes, we must remember that Jesus defeated ALL trouble and that we have His help. The key is to set our eyes on the source of our help. Remember, He is the source of your help!

Many times, trouble can be so overwhelming that you may be tempted to forget that your help comes from the Lord. The devil may attack with fear and attempt to pull you into a state of panic so that you rely on your own strength rather on God. At these times, you must remember that the Lord who made heaven and earth is your helper. If the One who crafted the heavens and the earth is your protector, you are guaranteed of safety. He has you covered, so you must keep your eyes fixed on HIM and not on the trouble. You have aid from the Maker and Creator of everything and He has promised to watch over you. In other words, God will not leave you unattended. HIS EYES ARE ON YOU!

The psalmist David was confident that God would cover him and keep him out of reach when trouble comes (Psalm 27:5). When the devil attempts to torment you during times of trouble, say, "Devil, I am out of reach because I am hidden in the secret place, according to the Word of God!" Then wait on the Lord –expect Him to protect you because He is your shield, your guard, your defense. Keep your confidence in the Lord and keep your eyes lifted toward the hills!

MANNA MOMENT: Identify 3 major distractions that cause you to take your eyes off Jesus, the source of your help.

My Portion

"This I recall to my mind, Therefore I have hope. Through the Lord's mercies we are not consumed, Because His compassions fail not. They are new every morning; Great is Your faithfulness. "The Lord is my portion," says my soul, "Therefore I hope in Him!"

Lamentations 3:21-24 NKJV

"Whom have I in heaven but You? And there is none upon earth that I desire besides You. My flesh and my heart fail; but God is the strength of my heart and my portion forever."

Psalm 73:25-26 NIV

"The Lord is my portion!" What does this statement mean to you, especially in the time of trouble? When the Bible speaks of the Lord being our portion it relates to our belonging to God; being in covenant with Him; and it can also refer to one's share, inheritance, or supply. In times of distress, knowing that God is your portion generates hope as it did for the prophet, Jeremiah. In Lamentations, Chapter 3, Jeremiah rehearsed his woes and remembered the hardships that he encountered as a prophet. Amid his lamenting, he has a spiritual *"Aha"* moment and remembers the unfailing love of the Lord and that it is only the mercy of God that protected him from annihilation. Hope rose in the prophet when he recalls the mercy and faithfulness of God. Then he declared that because the Lord was his "portion" or source of supply, he could wait or place his expectation in the Lord.

If God is your portion–your inheritance–your supply, you have no need to fear because God is everlasting and all-sufficient. If you look to earthly sources or if your inheritance derives from man, then it is limited at best. However, when you know that the Lord is your portion, then you can be assured that you have whatever you need, whenever you need it, and in whatever amount is required. There is no shortage or expiration on the supply. HE is your everlasting portion and his supply will never run out. In other words, you have an inheritance that results from being in covenant relationship with God through his Son, Jesus Christ. Therefore, you can expect God to supply EVERYTHING you need. If you need a supply of peace, provision, or protection, you can expect God to provide. If you need healing, you can hope in the Lord and confidently anticipate your supply of healing. Because the Lord is your supply, you can wait on Him with full assurance because He never fails. He is your portion forever and ever!

MANNA MOMENT: How does knowing that the Lord is your portion change your ability to wait on Him?

Never Give Up

"Then He spoke a parable to them, that men always ought to pray and not lose heart."

Luke 18:1 NKJV

Do not stop praying, no matter how things look. You may be tired, but do not give up. That is what Jesus told His disciples, "Do not give up!" When the answer to prayer is not realized immediately, you may become weary and feel like fainting. It is no wonder that Jesus took the time to encourage the disciples about the importance of continuing in prayer. He would not instruct them to persevere if their prayers were not effective. Likewise, your prayers are powerful, and will profit much if you do not give up. Jesus knew that there would be times when you would not feel like praying, when you would be tired physically or emotionally, or times when you would be discouraged. So, he took the time to encourage us to pray and not give up.

From the account in Luke 18, you can see that boldness and persistence are important ingredients of prayer. In this incident, there is a woman who went back repeatedly before an unjust judge asking for justice against her enemy. She went repeatedly before this judge who did not fear God and had no regard for man. This continual coming is called importunity, which demonstrates her persistence. Finally, the judge granted her request. The judge's explanation for granting the request was that he did not want to be worn out by her persistence. This woman was bold and determined.

She would not allow the judge's harshness to stop her. As a result, she received her request.

If this woman could go before an UNJUST judge and receive justice because of her persistence, surely your Heavenly Father will respond to your need. As you pray according to His will and continue to ask, seek, and knock (Luke 11:9-10), He will grant your request. Your Father wants to respond to your cries and grant you the petitions that you ask of Him. Just *NEVER GIVE UP!*

MANNA MOMENT: Have you stopped asking, seeking, and knocking? If so, identify 5 petitions that you will re-present to the Lord.

Quiet Confidence

"It is good that one should hope and wait quietly for the salvation of the Lord."

Lamentations 3:26 NKJV

"Wait on the Lord; be of good courage, and He shall strengthen your heart."

Psalm 27:14 NKJV

Would you agree that waiting is one of the greatest challenges in life? When you really want something and there is a delay, it is easy to become anxious, frustrated, or discouraged. You may find it challenging to maintain a confident attitude during the process. While waiting on the Lord, you must maintain a certain posture until the end, a courageous and expectant posture. Waiting on the Lord requires that you have full assurance that God will keep His Word. When you fix your mind of the truth that God's Word is reliable, your hope is awakened.

Hoping in God quiets your soul. According to the Bible, hope stabilizes or anchors the soul (mind, will, emotions). Thus, while you are waiting, we can be free of doubt, restlessness, and fear. We can be still and peaceful, confident that God will faithfully come through. You can be sure when waiting on Him because He is dependable. God has a flawless history of reliability. He has never missed an appointment and He has never lied. God will never stand you up or "no show" for His appointment with you. Therefore, you can rest and enjoy the wait as you focus on His promises.

When you concentrate on God's promises, your confidence level will soar. Whatever you focus on is what becomes largest in your mind. So, allow His promises to expand in your heart and mind so that you can confidently wait. Then remember that he ALWAYS keeps His WORD. Allow God's peace to saturate your thoughts and emotions despite what happens around you. Be assured that God will provide the strength that you need to hold on until He shows up in whatever way you need. You will never ever be disappointed if you keep your hope in God. When He comes, He will fulfill and even exceed your expectations.

MANNA MOMENT: Identify 3 things that you expect from God. List 5 ways that you will maintain confidence as you wait patiently for Him.

Relief Please!

"Hear me when I call, O God of my righteousness! You have relieved me in my distress; have mercy on me and hear my prayer."

Psalm 4:1 NKJV

"Do not hide Your face from me in the day of my trouble; Incline Your ear to me; In the day that I call, answer me speedily."

Psalm 102:2 NKJV

"I called on the Lord in distress; The Lord answered me and set me in a broad place."

Psalm 118:5 NKJV

What do you do when hardship comes? What is your first response to troubling situations? How do you handle the mental anguish that accompanies severe life challenges? Do you panic, retreat, become immobile, or do you turn to God as David, the psalmist did? Distress equates to mental suffering. Circumstances which cause distress occur frequently and usually unexpectedly so there is seldom time to prepare. There is not time to rehearse or contemplate what you will do or perfect how you will deal with the trouble. Affliction does not call for an appointment or wait to be scheduled. It just arrives – unannounced and uninvited. You must be connected to your source of relief before trouble comes. Your first response should be to do as David did – cry out to the Lord.

In times of distress, David turned to God in anticipation that he would receive a release from the trouble that he was experiencing. He was not tentative in approaching God for the removal of the source of the distress. It is the will of God for you to have the same level of confidence when you are in a season of distress. David drew upon his history with God and petitioned him fully expecting God to move on his behalf. Notice that David made extremely specific requests when asking for help. He asked God to:

- Answer him quickly
- Give him relief
- Be merciful to him
- Hear his prayer

Does this not describe the response that we want from God today? When we are engulfed in the complexity of a crisis, do we not want an answer right now? When the suffering is intense, we often feel like we cannot take anymore. We want a quick answer – speedy relief. Relief is like a break – a pause – rest from the affliction. That is what David was asking of God. He needed breathing space a time to recover from the trouble. Then David needed God's mercy – His kindness. He needed God to "pity" or to have compassion on his situation.

Finally, David, needed God to "hear" his prayer. He needed God's ear. There was a knowing that if God heard, then God would move and thus remove the distress. Repeatedly we see in scripture how David prayed this prayer and God delivered him. Your testimony can be the same as David's. As you cry out to God is distress, He will hear you and deliver you to a safe wide-open space where you can "catch your breath." He will set you in a large space where trouble cannot hem you in.

MANNA MOMENT: Identify areas where you need relief and cry to God like David.

Rescue 911

"Let the redeemed of the Lord say so, whom He has redeemed from the hand of the enemy,"

Psalm 107:2 NKJV

One of the greatest expressions of praise to our God is to let people know that we have been rescued from the enemy. This is what the children of Israel were doing in Psalm 107. This is their song of praise after being delivered from captivity by God Almighty. They sang about being REDEEMED. To be redeemed is to be released from captivity after a price is paid for your release. It is like a ransom that is paid for one who is in the hands of a kidnapper. When you are rescued from the enemy, you are freed from danger or any harm that was present. You are no longer under the power of the one who held you captive. In Psalm 107, the people are rejoicing because they were free from the power of their oppressor. They were rescued from bondage and they were NOT being quiet about it. They are telling those who have been redeemed to speak out.

Are you redeemed? Have you been rescued from a binding situation? Then speak out! Has God delivered you from the hand of the enemy? Let others know that your oppressor no longer has the right nor the power to control you. You are no longer under the power of sin and you have been released from whatever the enemy was using to hold you captive. You have been ransomed and brought to a place of safety. Now it is time to sing your song of deliverance just like the children of Israel did. They were so overjoyed to have their freedom back that they were shouting about it and singing about it. They were celebrating their freedom. God has broken the hold that the devil had on you. The enemy has no more claim or legal right to keep you enslaved. Your freedom is secure, and now it is time to SAY SO. Come forth with boldness and proclaim your liberty. Let God know that you appreciate the mercy that He extended toward you by paying the price for you to be free. Show your appreciation to Him by thanking Him for the BLOOD OF JESUS that paid the ransom for you to walk free of the enemy's power. Declare the goodness of the Lord to others by letting them know that He not only rescued you, but that He has also rescued them.

MANNA MOMENT: What was the danger that you were rescued from when Christ found you?

Safe in Him

"The name of the Lord is a strong tower; the righteous run to it and are safe."

Proverbs 18:10 NKJV

Every child has a need for safety and protection. We are no different as children of God. There are times in our lives when we feel unsafe and insecure. One of the worst experiences we can encounter is a lack of safety. We can feel unsafe concerning our health, finances, in a relationship, emotionally or physically. At these times, it is comforting to know there is a place where we can be safe and secure – protected from harm.

The Bible tells us that we must come to God as little children. Think about that. We are to relate to God our Father with the confidence and reliance of a little child assured that He will keep us safe from every danger. He is our loving Father, and we are his dependent children. When we feel insecure, uncertain, fearful, or overwhelmed, there is a place of refuge that is always available to us. That place is His name!

The Lord's name is a STRONG tower. A tower stands high above its surroundings and can be used as a look out point to see danger that is approaching. Well, the Name of The Lord is just like that. The Lord's Name is higher than anything and will serve as an overlook for anything that threatens us. There is safety in HIS NAME. What this means is that His name (reputation) should give us a sense of security. When feeling unsafe, it is important to remember and even meditate on the reputation of the Lord.

A person's reputation is established based upon what he or she does repeatedly—habits – characteristics – repeated behaviors over time. God has a track record of rescuing us from danger, a track record of being faithful, and a history of keeping His promises. So, whenever we need protection, we are to RUN to HIS NAME. Run there in your mind, in your thoughts, and remember His reputation is constant, because He does not change. Because He does not change, He will always be a strong tower. Therefore, anyone who has received Jesus as Savior qualifies for the safety, security, and protection that is found in His name.

How glorious it is to know that we always are protected if we "run to the Tower". We have a hiding place – a haven – a shelter from the storms of life. Take time today to call on the Name of the Lord and RUN into that strong tower.

MANNA MOMENT: Pray and ask the Lord to show you anything that causes you to feel unsafe and journal about God's reputation concerning those things. Saturate your mind with His reputation.

The Secret Place

"He that dwelleth in the secret place of the Most High shall abide under the shadow of the Almighty."

Psalm 91:1 KJV

There is no better place to dwell than in the "secret place." We must take heed to where we choose to dwell. Your dwelling place affects your state of mind and therefore the quality of your life. To dwell means to remain or to reside. This speaks of environment or surroundings. The atmosphere or setting that is around you affects who you are as well as your behavior. The Word of the Lord tells you that your environment should be the "secret place." The "secret place" is in the presence of the Lord. That is the place where you should reside. The "secret place" is so named because it is a special place that only those who have submitted their lives to Christ can go. It is not for those who have not yielded their hearts to Him.

The "secret place" represents shelter and divine protection. It is the place where you remain in Him. God promises that if you will abide there, He will shield you from danger, disease, and destruction. You have no need to fear. When you are in the safe environment of the Lord Most High, it dispels all fear. In the atmosphere of His protection, you are assured that He will cover you. If you make the Lord your habitation, you can be confident that He has assigned angels to protect you and keep you in all your ways. The Lord pledged that He will be with you in trouble and keep you safe IF you stay in "the secret place."

As you remain in the "secret place" remember the Name of the Lord and call on that name. Then the Lord will honor you, satisfy you, and show you his saving power. That saving power includes security, safety, soundness, wholeness, and preservation. You have open access to this dwelling place, and you never need to leave. You can forever be there because it is not a physical place. It is a spiritual location that only the righteous can enter. This place is one that is accessed with the heart through intimacy with the Most High God. You enter through prayer, reading and meditating in and on His Word, worship, thanksgiving, and faith in Him. You can live in this place and be forever safe under the shadow of His wings.

MANNA MOMENT: Identify 3 areas where you need God's protection and talk with Him about those needs.

Stand Firm

"But thanks be to God, who gives us the victory through our Lord Jesus Christ. Therefore, my beloved brethren, be steadfast, immovable, always abounding in the work of the Lord, knowing that your labor is not in vain in the Lord."

1 Corinthians 15:57-58 NKJV

Life presents a multitude of opportunities to be shaken, shifted, or sidetracked from the work of the Lord. At any given time, major life events ranging from death to unemployment find their way into the lives of believers. These situations present themselves unexpectedly and often repeatedly. Coping with them requires spiritual stamina or staying power. Without resilience there would be no way to rise above the circumstances that come to bring about your demise. One thing that is certain is that God would not command you to stand firm if He had not given you tools with which to do it. You have everything that you need to enable you to maintain your footing in God. There are specific instructions from the above verses that will enable you to remain steadfast, namely:

1. Watch! Be alert to see the enemy from afar.
2. Be courageous and strong in the power that God supplies.
3. Pour love into everything you do.
4. Decide that you WILL NOT move.
5. Work for the Lord with all your heart.

Following these directives from the Word of God will stabilize you and make you unshakeable no matter what winds blow in your life.

Satan's goal is to stop your progress and to hinder you from moving forward in the work of the Lord. If he can successfully throw you off balance, then his objective has been met. But you can stand firm when you remember that what you do for the Lord is of great value and is never unproductive or ineffective. What you do for the Lord counts. It is meaningful and important in His overall plan.

Do not underestimate your part in Kingdom work. The impact of what you do may not be visible immediately, but do not cease to give your absolute best. You may or may not receive recognition here on earth but stay on course to the end. Continue to serve the Lord with gladness of heart, knowing that your service to Him is being noted in Heaven.

MANNA MOMENT: What 3 main tactics does the enemy use to move you off your spiritual position? Identify 3 tools to address each of these tricks.

Stand Still

"And Moses said to the people, "Do not be afraid. Stand still, and see the salvation of the Lord, which He will accomplish for you today. For the Egyptians whom you see today, you shall see again no more forever. The Lord will fight for you, and you shall hold your peace."

Exodus 14:13-14 NKJV

"Be still and know that I am God; I will be exalted among the nations, I will be exalted in the earth!"

Psalms 46:10 NKJV

Movement is often our greatest enemy. Activity ... busyness.... motion can be the greatest hindrances to experiencing the fullness of our salvation. This is especially true when we faced with intimidating situations or times of adversity. At these times, it can be difficult to simply "be still" and allow God to fight for us. Often, fear tries to force its way to center stage and compete against the Word of God. This is a natural human response, but we can always rely on God's supernatural help. When Moses led the Israelites out of bondage, and the Egyptian army was pursuing them, he told the people to "be still". God parted the Red Sea and they walked through it on dry ground, but saw their enemies drowned.

In 2 Chronicles 20, King Jehoshaphat was being pursued by three armies. As the leader, he was at a loss as to what to do. The people looked to their king for direction. At this critical point, King Jehoshaphat made a profound statement in his prayer to God, "We do not know what to do, but our eyes are upon you." 2 Chronicles 20:12 (NIV). This leader began to seek the Lord and led the people in fasting. He also called them to prayer and worship and sought the counsel of God's prophet. The Lord spoke to King Jehoshaphat and the people, assuring them that it was HIS battle. He gave them 3 simple instructions: 1) stand still and see My salvation; 2) do not fear; and 3) go out against the enemy. With these instructions, the Lord assured them of His presence.

In obedience to God's command, King Jehoshaphat appointed those who would sing and praise the Lord to go out first ahead of the army. The praise was so powerful that their enemies became confused, turned on each other, and ultimately destroyed one another. The people of God did not fight in the battle. They praised! As a result, they experienced God's saving power. Perhaps God is saying to you, "Be still." Stop thinking, problem solving, laboring, worrying, and controlling things with all your activity. Be still, praise me, and I will confuse all your enemies.

MANNA MOMENT: What major battle(s) are you fighting that the Lord wants to fight for you? Be still and praise!

Steadfast Faith

"But the fruit of the Spirit is love, joy, peace, longsuffering, gentleness, goodness, faith, meekness, temperance: against such there is no law."

Galatians 5:22-23 KJV

The fruit described as faith actually deals with the characteristic of faithfulness. It is not really addressing the kind of faith that you would exert when trusting in or relying on something. Rather, this concept is faithfulness, meaning the quality of being reliable. It refers to traits like loyalty, fidelity, and allegiance. These are features that are necessary to have true relationships whether it is our relationship with God or with others. Faithfulness is vital if the relationship is to thrive.

We all want our relationships to stand the test of time. It is important to us for our friends and relatives to be loyal. A faithful or loyal person will not betray or desert us no matter how tough things get. When you have a loyal friend, he or she is steadfast and unswerving. You know that they are with you. A faithful friend is constant. There is no need to wonder about whether you can depend upon him or her because they have a track record of being solid. This is what God requires of us. He has proven His faithfulness to us. Now He wants us to be faithful to Him as well as to others.

Faithfulness should never be conditional. You ARE faithful. So BE faithful. When we are unreliable and wishy-washy, God continues to be unswerving in His character toward us. He forgives no matter what. He loves no matter what. He gives no matter what. When we are unreliable, God remains reliable. He is just loyal and constant in being who He is.

Jesus was faithful even during the hour of His betrayal. We should do no less. When we yield our lives to Christ, we must take on His nature and His character. Faithfulness is an attribute that we must cultivate if we are going to be devoted followers of Christ. The Holy Spirit is working this virtue in us even when we do not feel like anything is happening. Situations will arise that will test your faithfulness. You can pass the test with the aid of God's Spirit. Do not waver. Show God that He can rely on you!

MANNA MOMENT: Ask God to forgive you for times when you have been unfaithful to Him. Now forgive specific people who have been unfaithful to you. Call them by name and release them.

Tempted Yet Triumphant I

"Then Jesus was led up by the Spirit into the wilderness to be tempted by the devil. And when He had fasted forty days and forty nights, afterward He was hungry. Now when the tempter came to Him, he said, "If You are the Son of God, command that these stones become bread." But He answered and said, "It is written, 'Man shall not live by bread alone, but by every word that proceeds from the mouth of God.'"

Matthew 4:1-4 NKJV

Would you follow the Holy Spirit into a desolate place if you knew that intense temptation was ahead? Well, Jesus did just that and while in a vulnerable state; He was weak and hungry. Nevertheless, he remained strong in Spirit. Attempting to take advantage of Jesus' vulnerable physical state, the devil launched an attack against Jesus' identity using a powerful two-letter word, "if". Satan took the opportunity to attack the identity of Jesus by tempting Jesus to prove that he was the Messiah. This remains one of his commonly used tricks. He wants to tempt you to question your God-given identity and position in Jesus Christ, thereby causing you to doubt your gifts, talents, and purpose.

The devil brings up "ifs" that cause you to question who you are, what you are entitled to, and what you can do. Has he ever brought "ifs" to your mind when you are about to take a major step that will bring growth, promotion, or move you deeper into the will of God? He commonly uses thoughts like, "If you do that, you will fail." Or "If you do that, people will think...". The list goes on! However, we can rejoice in the truth that God also uses "ifs". The word "if" appears over 1500 times in the Scripture depending upon the Bible translation. In fact, God's promises are often preceded, by "if". Responding to God's "ifs" positions us for blessings. On the other hand, the devil's "ifs" lead to some level of destruction.

If Jesus had taken the devil's "dare," He would have tested God, and Satan would have thwarted God's plan for our deliverance. Instead, Jesus used the Word as a spiritual weapon to overcome temptation once again. Satan tried to use the Word of God against the Christ, but his tactics failed. Jesus resisted all three temptations and came out refreshed. Follow Jesus' example, so that you emerge victoriously from your wilderness experience!

MANNA MOMENT: Identify 3 things that challenge your obedience to God?

Tempted Yet Triumphant II

"Then Jesus, being filled with the Holy Spirit, returned from the Jordan, and was led by the Spirit into the wilderness, being tempted for forty days by the devil. And in those days, He ate nothing, and afterward, when they had ended, He was hungry. And the devil said to Him, "If You are the Son of God, command this stone to become bread." But Jesus answered him, saying, "It is written, 'Man shall not live by bread alone, but by every word of God.'"

Luke 4:1-4 NKJV

Just after Jesus was baptized in water and filled with the Holy Spirit, the Holy Spirit led Him into the wilderness to be tempted by the devil. Jesus spent a forty-day period in the wilderness fasting and praying. At the end of the temptation, a time of great hunger and weakness, Satan came to tempt Him. When your adversary, the devil, comes to you with temptation, you can be sure that He will look for an area of weakness as his point of entry. It is critical for you to know your points of weakness and shut off access to the devil. Jesus was in a vulnerable position physically, but His spirit was strong. For our benefit, Jesus demonstrated how to respond when temptation comes.

Notice what Satan used as the first method of temptation. He came to Jesus enticing Him with physical food. He wanted Jesus to use His power to do something contrary to the will of God – turn the stone to bread. It would have been a small thing for Jesus to create food, but His desire was to do the will of the Father. In no certain terms, Jesus made it clear that it was the Words from the mouth of the Father that gave Him life. Jesus quoted the Word of God that Moses spoke to the children of Israel as they wandered in the wilderness for forty years. Look at the pattern that Jesus provided for triumphing in the wilderness:

- He immediately recalled the Word of God. "*It is written...*"
- He declared the Word of God with His mouth.
- He acknowledged God (and His words) as His source of life.

Temptation exposes the contents of the heart, and Jesus' heart was completely pure. Our quest should be for our heart to become purer each day. Let us pray that our hearts be found pure in the day of our wilderness temptation.

MANNA MOMENT: Ask the Lord to reveal anything in your heart that would hinder you from submitting to HIM.

Tempted Yet Triumphant III

"Then he brought Him to Jerusalem, set Him on the pinnacle of the temple, and said to Him, "If You are the Son of God, throw Yourself down from here. For it is written: He shall give His angels charge over you, To keep you,' and, 'In their hands they shall bear you up, lest you dash your foot against a stone.' And Jesus answered and said to him, "It has been said, 'You shall not tempt the LORD your God.'" Now when the devil had ended every temptation, he departed from Him until an opportune time."

Luke 4:9-13 NKJV

Jesus remained unswerving during intense temptations in the wilderness. He stayed on course knowing that the Father was with Him. His complete submission to God's will is clearly demonstrated by Jesus' response to the devil's schemes. Jesus was dedicated to completing the assignment that the Father had given Him, namely death on the cross to redeem mankind with His precious blood. It is obvious that the devil was bent on preventing this from happening. The reality is that the plan of God could not be stopped! This account of Jesus' time of temptation should encourage you to resist the devil and remain focused on God's plan for your life. Satan's goal is to stop you from fulfilling the will of God, but the Word of God will defeat the devil and cause him to flee.

When Satan tempted Jesus, he inserted and emphasized the word "if" to challenge Jesus' identity, by saying "*'if'* *you are the Son of God...*" Using scripture (Psalms 91:11-12) to challenge Jesus, he hoped that Jesus would accept his challenge. Satan knew that if Jesus hurled Himself down and the angels rescued Him, the people would believe that Jesus was the Messiah. This would "spoil" the redemption plan built upon Jesus going to the cross and shedding His blood. It is true that the Word of God promises that His angels will keep us in all our ways, but we must never test God by doing things contrary to His will. For this reason, Jesus once again quoted the Word of God, (Deuteronomy 6:16). This verse instructs us not to test the Lord God. The evil one will use any tactic, even the Word of God, to move you away from God's will. He will try to use God's Word against you and to mock your God-given identity. Like Jesus, you must use the Word of God to overcome the devil's temptations and continue to do the will of God. If you follow Jesus' example, you can count on God to refresh you and bring you out of the wilderness victoriously!

MANNA MOMENT: Identify 3 spiritual insights that you received from Jesus' experience in the wilderness.

The Quiet Soul

"You will keep him in perfect peace, whose mind is stayed on You, because he trusts in You."

Isaiah 26:3 NKJV

It seems that the world around us is becoming more and more clamorous with each passing day. There is an abundance of activity, noise, and all kinds of information continually coming at us. All these factors affect the soul's ability to find the quietness that it needs. It is wonderful to know that despite all the busyness and clamor that the soul can still find rest. God has made provision for your soul to have the quietness that it needs.

The way the soul finds rest is by being "stayed" on the Lord. When the Word of God speaks of your mind being "stayed" on Him it is not referring to our thoughts being focused on God every single moment. This would be impossible since you have other responsibilities that require thought. The principle is much broader than that. Your mind being "stayed" on Him is descriptive of the state or core of your thought life. In other words, the foundation of your thought life should be built upon and around the Lord and His Word. Your mind should be fixed or established in agreement with the nature and character of God. When this is the case, the result is PERFECT (complete) PEACE.

Peace is marked by a state of tranquility in the soul even in the face of outer turmoil. The peace is that which Jesus spoke of when He said, *"Peace I leave with you. My peace I give to you, not as the world gives do I give to you. Let not your heart be troubled; neither let it be afraid."* (John 14:27 NKJV).

The peace that Jesus gave you is unlike the peace that comes from the world in that it never falls short. It is pure and never disappoints. What the world offers is a false sense of peace that cannot bring true rest for the soul. It is imperfect, but the perfect peace that Jesus gives lacks nothing. The peace that He gives to you can never be taken away.

MANNA MOMENT: What spiritual tool will you utilize to keep your mind stayed on the Lord today?

The Refiner's Fire

"You have caused men to ride over our heads; We went through fire and through water; but You brought us out to rich fulfillment."

Psalm 66:12 NKJV

"Behold, I have refined you, but not as silver; I have tested you in the furnace of affliction."

Isaiah 48:10 NKJV

Your faith is very precious to God. According to the Bible, it is more precious than gold or silver. Much like silver and gold, your faith must go through a purifying process. If these precious metals are going to be pure, they must be refined. This refining process requires heat. Your faith is like gold that must go through cycles of heating and cooling for the impurities to be removed. All this must happen for the gold to shine. Likewise, your faith will not shine until it goes through cycles of testing. As your faith undergoes these cycles anything that will pollute or contaminate it is removed. Refining is an intense process but a necessary one for your faith to come forth in its purest form.

When gold is refined, it is typically exposed to heat at extremely high temperatures. Often fire is used until the gold melts. In some processes, the gold is then exposed to chemicals such as gases or acids until the desired level of purity is reached. Some methods require that the gold be frozen after being melted – extreme changes in conditions. Typically, when the refining process is complete, the gold is separated from any other metals or contaminants. The impurities rise to the top like a layer of scum and are skimmed off and discarded.

God is the master refiner and He will test you- but He will not test you with sin. He will test you in the furnace so that you can come out free of pollution. The trials that come will bring the necessary heat to rid you of anything that will hinder your faith from shinning like gold. The Lord has His own oven and He will turn up the heat in order that you may be separated as one whose faith has stood the test. The Word of God says that He sits as the Refiner. His desire is that you will excel and endure every temptation that you experience. Others will observe you as you are being tested and tried. When they see your faith shining brightly, it will bring much glory to the Lord God. If you submit to the refining process, you will be able to stand before HIM with great confidence. Stay in the furnace until THE REFINER completes the work of bringing forth the gold in you.

MANNA MOMENT: How is THE REFINER turning up the heat in your life currently? Name 3 specific things.

Trust During Trouble

"Trust in the Lord with all your heart and lean not on your own understanding; In all your ways acknowledge Him, And He shall direct your paths."

Prov. 3:5-6 NKJV

When you are going through tough times, you need to trust that God is with you, and that He will guide through the stormy seasons of life. Trust should be the foundation of every relationship, especially our relationship with God. Everything concerning our relationship with Him must be built upon trust or the relationship cannot thrive. To trust means to have confidence in and depend upon the character, strength, or truth of someone or something. Our relationship with God is based upon our having trusted in His Son, Jesus Christ. This trust must be demonstrated during the good, bad, and ugly seasons of our lives.

We are commanded to trust in the Lord with our entire heart and not to trust in or rely on ourselves. God has a reputation of being trustworthy because He always keeps His promises and His character never changes. Therefore, we can depend upon Him, especially in trying times. Our confidence in Him should be unwavering because He has never, nor will He ever, fail to keep His word. Because of this we can safely trust in Him. God will always uphold His reputation and be true to His nature. So, do not lose hope no matter what life presents! Your faithful Father is with you!

You can always trust God in every area. That is why you must acknowledge Him in ALL your ways – in every matter of life. IF you depend upon Him and look to Him in every area, He will give you direction – guaranteed! Let go of your own understanding (which is limited) and rely on God's infinite wisdom. Do not accept less than God's best during times of adversity. Depend upon Him and be assured that He will point you to the right path and give you grace to overcome!

MANNA MOMENT: Name 3 situations that will you trust God with today so that you can get HIS results?

Under the Shelter

"He who dwells in the secret place of the Most High Shall abide under the shadow of the almighty. I will say of the Lord, "He is my refuge and my fortress; my God, in Him I will trust."

Psalm 91:1-4 NKJV

There is a place of rest for all who abide under the shelter of the Most High God. Protection and security are promised to us if we dwell in His presence and place our trust in Him. God promised to cover those who live under His covering. The word "surely" indicates the certainty of this protection if we stay in this safe place. This secret place is the believer's place of refuge from trouble, danger, and harm. This is a guaranteed haven if we remain under His wings. Moving from under the covering makes us vulnerable to the onslaught of the enemy and gives the adversary access to us, our families, marriages, jobs, health, finances, etc. Therefore, we must find the secret place and make it our permanent home.

You may wonder what or where is this secret place? How do I remain there? First, it is important to know that God wants to reveal the secret place to His children. He wants you to abide there, and HE made this "place" available to all who receive His Son. The secret place is God's presence, a spiritual place that is found by placing your trust in Jesus Christ. This place is described as secret because it is not seen or known by everyone. It is not understood by those who choose dwell elsewhere. The awesome thing is everyone is welcome and can enter in by simply choosing to trust in the Lord Jesus Christ.

The secret place is a mystery to those who remain married to the world and who rely on other resources for protection. On the other hand, this haven is open to those who love and trust the Lord. This revelation is available once one decides to yield to Christ. After choosing Christ, access is granted, and you can abide there forever. Through prayer, worship, study of and meditation upon the Word of God, and fellowship with the saints of God, we find the secret place. In that space, we are safe during trouble! That is the secret place!

MANNA MOMENT: Identify 5 people, places, or things that attempt to pull you out of the secret place. Confess them to God and ask for the grace and wisdom to overcome them. Obey what God reveals to you!

Unshakeable

"Lord, who may abide in Your tabernacle? Who may dwell in Your holy hill? He who walks uprightly, and works righteousness, and speaks the truth in his heart; he who does not backbite with his tongue, nor does evil to his neighbor, nor does he take up a reproach against his friend; in whose eyes a vile person is despised, but he honors those who fear the Lord; he who swears to his own hurt and does not change; he who does not put out his money at usury, nor does he take a bribe against the innocent. He who does these things shall never be moved."

Psalm 15:1-5 NKJV

How can we live in this world and not be shaken or lose our spiritual footing? When surrounded by increasing lawlessness, greed, corruption, violence, sickness, and countless forms of danger, how does one maintain stability? Well, there is a way that is outlined for those who trust in Christ Jesus to not be upset, stunned, or dazed by things from within or by external happenings. Often the same circumstance that affect those who live apart from Christ, also happen to Christians. For example, Christians will experience loss of employment, the death of loved ones, sickness and disease, financial loss, and other crises. The difference is that these situations are likely to devastate the unbeliever, but the believer must not be dismayed when these forms of adversity arise.

There is a way that believers can position themselves to be stable in times of trouble. Stability in tough times begins with living a righteous life which means walking in the fear of the Lord.

The reverential fear of the Lord provokes one to live a life of integrity which includes truth, sincerity, sameness, and a courageous heart. The Bible describes these individuals as those who are stable, fearless in times of trouble, and who prevail over their enemies. Those who are unshaken are memorable, leaving an impression. They are unforgettable. In other words, they are remembered as those who could not be thrown off track no matter what came their way. The Lord Jesus warned that in this world we would have suffering and hardship, but that we are not to lose heart. He assured us that He handled the trouble so that we can have joy. Those who follow the way outlined in God's word can abide in His tent and be welcomed into His presence. This type of believer will be known as *UNSHAKEABLE*.

MANNA MOMENT: List 2 current situations that threaten your stability? In writing, discuss how you will remain unshakeable.

When the Storm Rises

"And a great windstorm arose, and the waves beat into the boat, so that it was already filling. But He was in the stern, asleep on a pillow. And they awoke Him and said to Him, Teacher, do You not care that we are perishing?" Then He arose and rebuked the wind, and said to the sea, "Peace, be still!" And the wind ceased and there was a great calm. But He said to them, "Why are you so fearful? How is it that you have no faith?"

Mark 4:37-40 NKJV

Sometimes the circumstances of life can resemble unstable weather patterns or the conditions of a raging storm. Storms can be unsettling and even terrifying. When the winds are blowing, especially the winds of a hurricane or tornado, it is tempting to panic. The force of the wind becomes so great that fear is the first response. The danger of the storm is so overwhelming that you do not know what to do. This describes the situation that the disciples experienced when they were in the boat with Jesus. A violent storm came up, but Jesus was resting peacefully in the boat. The storm was all around them, but Jesus was in the boat with them. They became so afraid that they roused Jesus from His rest and accused Him of not caring that they were "perishing." To them, it felt like they were perishing. I am sure the situation looked like they were going to perish, BUT THEY WERE NOT ALONE.

When a violent storm rages in our lives, we often respond like the disciples did to the storm that they faced. Have you been faced with something so overwhelming that it feels like a hurricane just blew through your life? What did you do? You will no doubt face many more windstorms in your life, but remember:

- ➤ You are not alone. Just like Jesus was in the boat with the disciples, He will be with you in the storm.

- ➤ Jesus has power over your storm. All Jesus had to do was say, "Peace be still" and the wind ceased. He will speak to the winds in your life and will not allow them to destroy you. He will rebuke the wind for you.

- ➤ Keep the faith. Do not listen to voices that say you will perish. You are going THROUGH the storm not CAMPING OUT in it. The storm WILL pass over.

Hold onto these thoughts when you encounter the storms of life, and be mindful that the God, who has ALL POWER is there to speak peace to the wind and to the sea on your behalf. Do not be overcome with fear and hold onto Jesus until the storm passes over.

MANNA MOMENT: What 3 fears arise concerning the current storm(s) in your life?

When Trouble Comes

"For in the time of trouble He shall hide me in His pavilion; in the secret place of His tabernacle He shall hide me; He shall set me high upon a rock."

Psalm 27:5 NKJV

"These things I have spoken to you, that in Me you may have peace. In the world you will have tribulation; but be of good cheer, I have overcome the world."

John 16:33 NKJV

The world in which we live is filled with trouble. This is a fact. Trouble comes in various ways and in varying degrees of intensity. It comes at unexpected times and in unexpected ways and it is NEVER welcome. Jesus gave us a powerful assurance concerning this unpleasant reality. According to Jesus, we all will have trouble, distress, suffering, hardships, and pain. As you are reading this, you may be in great trouble. There may be a tragedy that you are dealing with or some other type of misfortune. If so… know this … It has ALREADY BEEN OVERCOME.

Jesus took special care to let you know what to expect from the world, and He also declared that He has conquered the world's system. As absurd as it seems, the solution that He gives is to be of good cheer. When you set your mind and heart on the truth that Jesus has triumphed over the world FOR YOU, that will cause you to be of good cheer. Trouble comes as oppression or pressure to weigh you down and to rob you of the joy of your salvation. However, it has no power over you when you decide to be of good cheer. This choice requires that you take your mind off the trouble and put it on the victory that Jesus won FOR YOU. Put your mind on the ONE who gave you the power to overcome.

In the Old Testament, David (the Psalmist) talks about having a "secret place" to go in the time of trouble. This gives us the picture of a tent or covering where you are safe from the trouble. There is a place where trouble cannot find you, and God will hide you there. There will be times when trouble may be looking for you, but it will not be able to locate you, because God will hide you from it. When you need to be lifted, God will raise you above the trouble so that it cannot reach you. You have a shelter from the storm, and you can have peace during trouble. Peace is yours because you are IN HIM. JESUS HAS ALREADY CONQUERED ALL OF YOUR TROUBLES!

MANNA MOMENT: What trouble(s) are you facing? Take time to rejoice that Jesus has already overcome them for you. Praise Him and be of good cheer!

Wilderness Seasons

"Then Jesus, being filled with the Holy Spirit, returned from the Jordan and was led by the Spirit into the wilderness, being tempted for forty days by the devil. And in those days, He ate nothing, and afterward, when they had ended, He was hungry."

Luke 4:1 NKJV

As Christians we sometimes experience wilderness seasons. We learn from the Word of God that even Jesus had to experience wilderness conditions for Him to fulfill the will of God. Throughout the Holy Scriptures, we see both individuals and nations spending time in both physical and spiritual wildernesses. These times ended in either their triumph or tragedy, depending upon how they negotiated those wilderness conditions. Likewise, your responses during your wilderness seasons will determine whether you emerge from the wilderness in victory.

The use of the metaphor of a physical wilderness will provide a backdrop for understanding a spiritual wilderness. The conditions are much the same. The most basic definition of a wilderness is a place that is typically barren and empty. It is generally lifeless – a desert that is void of vegetation. The wilderness is marked by heat, usually wild animals, sometimes mountains, and uncultivated land. It is not a place where we prefer to be. The interesting thing is that when God is about to move you to "higher ground" it often requires that you travel through the wilderness.

Wilderness experiences may also follow a season where you have had some of your most significant spiritual experiences. Such was the case with Jesus, our Savior. His wilderness experience occurred right after His baptism and before He began His powerful, public ministry. Wilderness experiences often come before movement into deeper levels of God's purpose for our lives. Perhaps this is the season you are in today. Here are some features of wilderness times:

- *Loneliness* – feelings of isolation or the need to withdraw
- *Dryness* – lack of productivity or fruitfulness
- *Rockiness* – obstacles, difficulties, troubles, unsteadiness
- *Emptiness* – difficulty finding satisfaction in key areas of your life
- *Temptation* – enticement and opportunity to yield to Satan's devices in your thoughts, word, or deeds

These are some tell-tale signs of a wilderness season. Maybe you are not there right now. If that is the case, prepare so that you will be fortified WHEN your season comes. On the other hand, if you are in the wilderness, REJOICE for it is the best time for the power of the Holy Spirit to work in your life. Determine NOW that you will not wander in the wilderness but that you will allow God's Spirit to lead you out in VICTORY. If you follow HIM, you WILL come out!

MANNA MOMENT: List 5 symptoms of your wilderness experience (past or present). Find a Scripture or biblical experience to address each symptom.

Reflections

My heart is filled with thanksgiving that you have spent forty days preparing your heart, mind, and spirit to face adversity with confidence. I pray that you were strengthened by the readings in this volume and that you have a clearer view of the reality of the victory that Jesus won for you on the cross. I encourage you to continue to be filled with hope, knowing that Jesus has overcome whatever you may face and that that God is with you in all your trouble, causing you to rise above it.

To those who may have read this book but have not experienced a personal relationship with Christ, I invite you to take that step today. You can do so by praying this simple prayer:

"Dear God, I believe that Jesus is your Son and that He died for my sins on the Cross. I ask you to forgive me for my sins, and I receive Jesus as my Lord and Savior. Thank you for hearing my prayer! Amen!"

If you took that step, you have new hope – eternal life! Be sure to find a church where you can grow and become more like Christ!

God bless you! I look forward to sharing the next volume of *MORNING MANNA MEDITATIONS* with you and other books intended to help you live the victorious life!

www.ingramcontent.com/pod-product-compliance
Lightning Source LLC
LaVergne TN
LVHW011731060526
838200LV00051B/3139